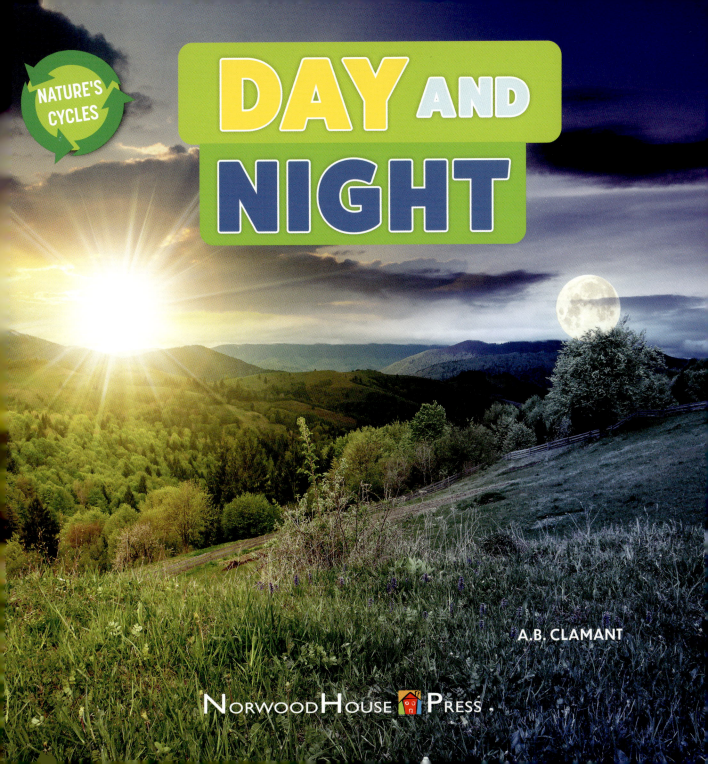

Cataloging-in-Publication Data

Names: Clamant, A.B., 1972-.
Title: Day and night / A.B. Clamant.
Description: Buffalo, NY : Norwood House Press, 2026. | Series: Nature's cycles | Includes glossary and index.
Identifiers: ISBN 9781978575554 (pbk.) | ISBN 9781978575561 (library bound) | ISBN 9781978575578 (ebook)
Subjects: LCSH: Day--Juvenile literature. | Night--Juvenile literature. | Earth (Planet)--Rotation--Juvenile literature.
Classification: LCC QB633.C536 2026 | DDC 525'.35--dc23

Published in 2026 by
Norwood House Press
2544 Clinton Street
Buffalo, NY 14224

Copyright © 2026 Norwood House Press
Designer: Rhea Magaro
Editor: Kim Thompson

Photo credits: Cover, p. 1 Mike Pellinni/Shutterstock.com; p. 3 Peter Sobhy/Shutterstock.com; p. 5 Ollyy/Shutterstock.com; p. 7 aastock/Shutterstock.com; p. 9 bluedog studio/Shutterstock.com; p. 11 IgorZh/Shutterstock.com; p. 12 phototrip2403/Shutterstock.com; p. 13 Vlad G/Shutterstock.com; p. 15 Saifullahphotopgrapher/Shutterstock.com; p. 16 DfgzPhoto/Shutterstock.com; p. 18 Arka1234/Shutterstock.com; p. 19 LUMIKK555/Shutterstock.com; p. 21 PeopleImages.com - Yuri A /Shutterstock.com

All rights reserved. No part of this book may be reproduced in any form without permission in writing from the publisher, except by a reviewer.

Printed in the United States of America

Some of the images in this book illustrate individuals who are models. The depictions do not imply actual situations or events.

CPSIA compliance information: Batch #CSNHP26: For further information contact Norwood House Press at 1-800-237-9932.

TABLE OF CONTENTS

What Causes Day and Night? 4

Earth Spins 7

Facing the Sun 10

One Whole Day 14

The Cycle Continues 20

Glossary 22

Thinking Questions 23

Index 24

About the Author 24

What Causes Day and Night?

Look outside. Do you see bright daylight or a black sky? Do you know why it gets light and dark each day? It happens because of the **cycle** of day and night.

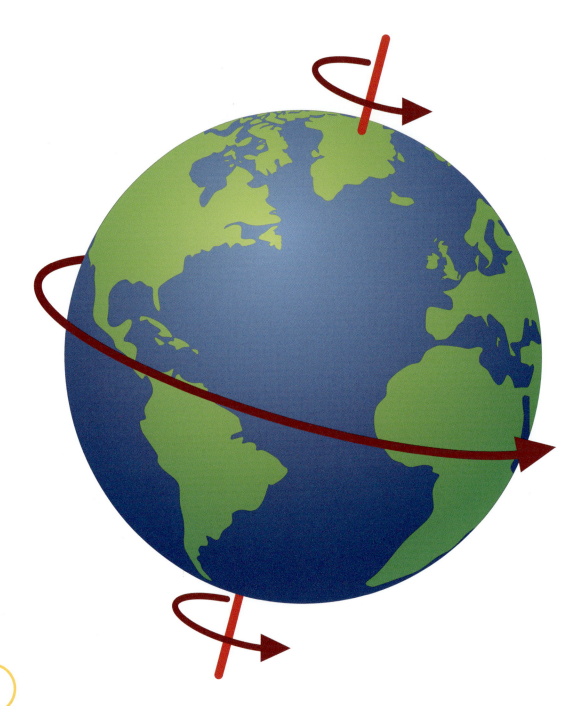

Earth Spins

Earth turns like a top. It is always **rotating** around its **axis**. Imagine a pole that runs from the top of the planet to the bottom. This imaginary line is an axis.

It takes 24 hours for Earth to make one complete rotation. There are 24 hours in one day.

Imagine: You wake up, stay busy all day, and go to bed. By the time you wake up again, the Earth has made one full turn.

Facing the Sun

As Earth rotates, one side of the planet faces the Sun. It gets the Sun's light and heat. The other side faces away from the Sun. It is darker and colder.

On one side of the world, it is daytime. On the other side of the world, it is nighttime.

12

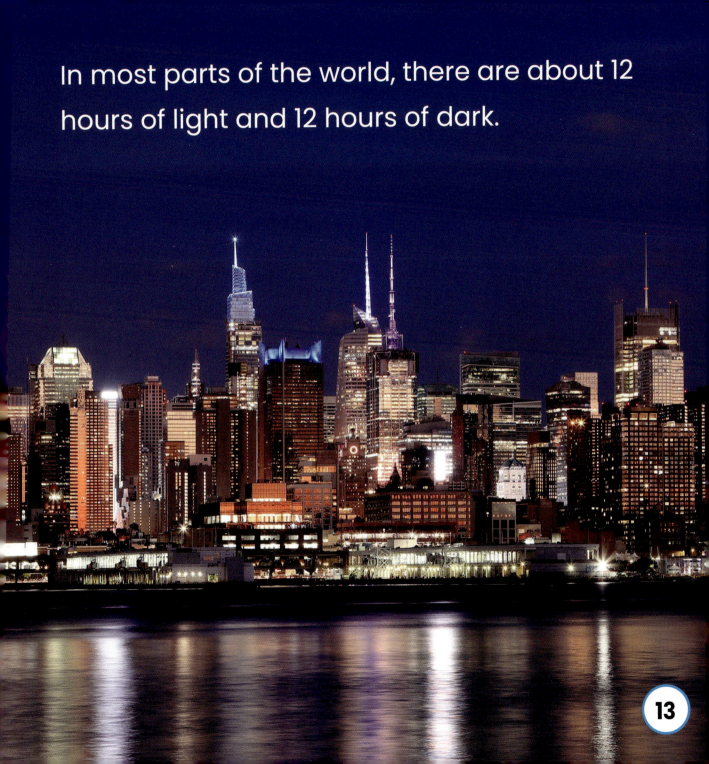

In most parts of the world, there are about 12 hours of light and 12 hours of dark.

One Whole Day

Dawn is the first bit of morning sunlight you see. It means your part of Earth is turning toward the Sun. Because Earth's rotation is **counterclockwise**, the Sun seems to "rise" in the east.

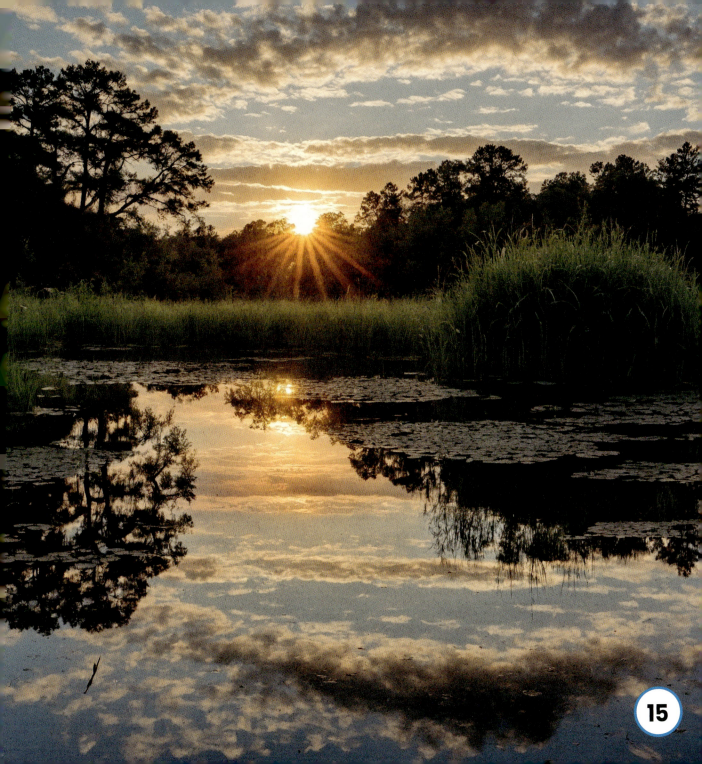

By **midday**, or noon, your part of Earth is directly facing the Sun. The Sun reaches its highest point in the sky. Then, it keeps moving across the sky.

At **dusk**, the Sun starts to disappear below the **horizon**. As your part of Earth turns away from the Sun, the Sun "sets" in the west.

At **midnight**, the night is halfway over. The sky is darkest. Your part of Earth is turned completely away from the Sun. But soon, the Sun will rise again.

The Cycle Continues

The next time you watch the Sun rise or set, remember what you are seeing. It is the cycle of day and night. Earth keeps turning to share the Sun with the rest of the world!

Glossary

axis (AK-sis): a real or imaginary line through the middle of an object, around which that object spins

counterclockwise (koun-tur-KLAHK-wize): in a direction opposite to the way the hands of a clock move

cycle (SYE-kuhl): a series of events that repeat over and over in the same order

dawn (dawn): the time of day just before the Sun rises

dusk (duhsk): the time of day just before night

horizon (huh-RYE-zuhn): the line where the land or ocean seems to meet the sky

midday (MID-day): the middle of the day; noon or 12:00 p.m.

midnight (MID-nite): the middle of the night; 12:00 a.m.

rotating (ROH-tay-ting): moving in a circle around a central point

Thinking Questions

1. Why does the Sun seem to move across the sky from east to west?

2. At what time of day is the Sun highest in the sky? Why?

3. How many hours are in one day? Why?

4. Why do you think the light is dim at dawn and dusk?

5. What is the darkest time of the day? Why?

Index

east 14

horizon 18

hours 8, 13

light 4, 10, 13, 14

midnight 19

noon 17

rise 14, 19, 20

rotation 7, 8, 10, 14

set 18, 20

west 18

About the Author

A.B. Clamant is the author of several fact-filled books for kids. The daughter of two grade school teachers, she developed a love of children's books at an early age. When she's not writing, she is working on opening her own petting zoo, ABCs Animals. Her favorite foods are bread, fruit strips, and candy. A.B. Clamant lives in Springfield, Missouri, with her four cats: Monkey, Corky, Prissy, and Nelly.